WALKI

NIDDER

Paul Hannon

HILLSIDE

HILLSIDE GUIDES - ACROSS THE NORTH

Long Distance Walks

- COAST TO COAST WALK
- DALES WAY
- CLEVELAND WAY
- WESTMORLAND WAY
- FURNESS WAY
- CUMBERLAND WAY
- LADY ANNE'S WAY
- PENDLE WAY
- NIDDERDALE WAY

Hillwalking - Lake District

- LAKELAND FELLS - SOUTH
- LAKELAND FELLS - EAST
- LAKELAND FELLS - NORTH
- LAKELAND FELLS - WEST

Circular Walks - Peak District

- NORTHERN PEAK
- EASTERN PEAK
- CENTRAL PEAK
- SOUTHERN PEAK
- WESTERN PEAK

Circular Walks - Yorkshire Dales

- HOWGILL FELLS
- THREE PEAKS
- MALHAMDALE
- WHARFEDALE
- NIDDERDALE
- WENSLEYDALE
- SWALEDALE

Circular Walks - North York Moors

- WESTERN MOORS
- SOUTHERN MOORS
- NORTHERN MOORS

Circular Walks - South Pennines

- BRONTE COUNTRY
- CALDERDALE
- ILKLEY MOOR

Circular Walks - Lancashire

- BOWLAND
- PENDLE & THE RIBBLE
- WEST PENNINE MOORS

Circular Walks - North Pennines

- TEESDALE
- EDEN VALLEY

Yorkshire Pub Walks

- HARROGATE/WHARFE VALLEY
- HAWORTH/AIRE VALLEY

Large format colour hardback

FREEDOM OF THE DALES

BIKING COUNTRY

- YORKSHIRE DALES CYCLE WAY
- WEST YORKSHIRE CYCLE WAY
- MOUNTAIN BIKING - WEST & SOUTH YORKSHIRE
- AIRE VALLEY BIKING GUIDE
- CALDERDALE BIKING GUIDE
- GLASGOW Clyde Valley & Loch Lomond

- YORK WALKS *City Theme Walks*

- WALKING COUNTRY TRIVIA QUIZ *Over 1000 questions*

Send for a detailed current catalogue and pricelist

NIDDERDALE WAY

Paul Hannon

HILLSIDE

HILLSIDE
PUBLICATIONS
11 Nessfield Grove
Keighley
West Yorkshire
BD22 6NU

First published 1998

© Paul Hannon 1998

ISBN 1 870141 64 4

Cover illustration: New Bridge, near Birstwith; Yorke's Folly
Back cover: On the Nidd's bank above Pateley Bridge
(Paul Hannon/Big Country Picture Library)

Page One: Idol Rock, Brimham
Page Three: Nidd Heads, Lofthouse

Printed in Great Britain by
Carnmor Print and Design
95-97 London Road
Preston
Lancashire
PR1 4BA

CONTENTS

Bewerley Grange Chapel

INTRODUCTION

The Nidderdale Way is a 53 mile waymarked walking route in North Yorkshire. Devised in the early 1980s, its popularity is such that it has found its way onto Ordnance Survey maps. The Way encircles the valley of the River Nidd by means of a wide and varied range of footpaths, bridleways and country roads, taking a course up one side of the valley and returning down the other. As such, the outward and return legs are never far apart, making it very accessible to the day walker: the finest means of tackling it, however, is as a four-day walk.

Though far from the least attractive of the Yorkshire Dales, Nidderdale is probably the least known of the major valleys. While the gateway towns of Harrogate and Knareborough receive ample attention, the dale itself remains largely free from congestion. In spite of this solitude, Nidderdale is renowned for a number of attractions, notably the natural features of Brimham Rocks and How Stean Gorge. Further up-dale are the holes of Goyden Pot and Manchester Hole, while the reservoirs of Scar House and Angram fill the dalehead in a bleak setting beneath high fells. Add to this Gouthwaite Reservoir, Yorke's Folly and Guise Cliff, the sleepy villages of Ramsgill and Wath, and it soon becomes clear why Nidderdale is such a jewel of the Dales.

Aside from natural rockscapes and man-made lakes, Nidderdale boasts two other outstanding aspects - heather and trees. The valley is little short of lavished with attractive woodland, while the heather moors reach endlessly over sweeping horizons. In the upper dale, much of this vast moorland is managed for grouse shooting. In monastic times the high moors dividing upper Nidderdale from the Kirkby Malzeard/Ripon district saw a busy passage of trade: monks and lay-workers would tramp their way over to markets there and to Fountains Abbey itself, laden with the fruits of their labours, largely in the form of lead and wool. Before passing to the abbeys of Fountains and Byland, the whole of Nidderdale was a Royal hunting chase.

All the area of this walk sits outside the Yorkshire Dales National Park, for the most part excluded from its original boundaries as a sop to water boards and private landowning interests. Nidderdale is the easternmost valley of the Yorkshire Dales, and it concedes nothing to its neighbours. Indeed, the vast majority of the Nidderdale Way is within the Nidderdale Area of Outstanding Natural Beauty, a belated recognition of the exceptional scenic qualities of this landscape.

6

Getting around

The only railway line in the area is that serving Harrogate. Bus services radiate from here, the principal one being up the Nidd Valley to Pateley Bridge. The Way's starting point at Ripley is served from Harrogate and Ripon. A lengthy section of the walk in the upper dale is served only by seasonal and school buses. The Way itself is largely well waymarked, though one couldn't hope to follow it by waymarks alone: some stages have a dearth of them while others seem to have unnecessary ones.

Using the guide

The route description begins at Ripley, with its various facilities, ample parking and, importantly, bus service. Tradition has the Way starting 2 miles away at Hampsthwaite, but both the location and the attractions of Ripley make it a far more rewarding start and finish. However, as the walk is circular, where you opt to join it is a matter of preference and convenience. The guide divides into four stages, each making an undemanding day's walk. No doubt some will choose to cover a longer distance within a good day's march. The intervening stages end at Pateley Bridge, Middlesmoor and Bewerley, though any number of permutations can be made. Indeed, such is the proximity of the outward and return legs, that the way easily divides into four circular walks, with the links at Smelthouses-Dacre Banks; Pateley Bridge-Bewerley; and Bouthwaite-Ramsgill. Another option would be two different weekends based at Pateley Bridge, doing the upper dale on one occasion, and the lower dale another time.

Each stage is self-contained, essential information being followed by a simple map and concise route description. Dovetailed between are notes of features along the way, and interspersed are illustrations which capture the flavour of the walk and document many items of interest. Essential route description has been highlighted in bold, in order to make it accessible amongst the other snippets of information. The sketch maps serve only to identify the location of the route, and whilst the description should be sufficient to guide one around, an Ordnance Survey map is recommended.

The entire route is highlighted on Explorer Map 26 *Nidderdale* (to be renumbered), and as such it is an indispensible companion to the guidebook. Additionally, at the scale of 1:50,000, Landranger sheet 99 *Northallerton & Ripon* covers most of the route (sheet 104 *Leeds, Bradford & Harrogate* covers part of the final stage), and is particularly useful for planning.

SOME USEFUL FACILITIES

A general guide only

	Accommodation	Bus service	Pub	Post office	Other shop	WC	Phone	Cafe
Ripley	•	•	•	•	•	•	•	•
Bishop Thornton	•	•	•				•	
Shaw Mills			•				•	
Burnt Yates	•	•	•				•	
Brimham Rocks			•			•		•
Low Laithe	•	•	•				•	
Glasshouses/Wilsill	•	•	•	•		•	•	•
Pateley Bridge	•	•	•	•	•	•	•	•
Wath	•	•	•				•	
Lofthouse	•	•	•	•		•	•	
Scar House			•			•		
Middlesmoor	•	•	•			•	•	•
How Stean		•			•	•	•	•
Ramsgill	•	•	•				•	
Bewerley	•	•	•				•	
Dacre Banks	•	•	•		•	•	•	
Summerbridge	•	•	•	•	•		•	•
Darley	•	•	•	•			•	•
Birstwith	•	•	•	•			•	
Hampsthwaite	•	•	•	•	•		•	•

THE COUNTRY CODE
Respect the life and work of the countryside
Protect wildlife, plants and trees
Keep to public paths across farmland
Safeguard water supplies
Go carefully on country roads
Keep dogs under control
Guard against all risks of fire
Fasten all gates
Leave no litter - take it with you
Make no unnecessary noise
Leave livestock, crops and machinery alone
Use gates and stiles to cross fences, hedges and walls

SOME USEFUL ADDRESSES

Ramblers' Association
1/5 Wandsworth Road, London SW8 2XX
Tel. 0171-339 8500

North Yorkshire County Council Public Rights of Way
Area 3 District, Croft House, Carleton Road, Skipton BD23 2BG
Tel. 01756-793344

Nidderdale AONB Project
18b, High Street, Pateley Bridge
Tel. 01423-712027

Tourist Information
14 High Street **Pateley Bridge** HG3 5AW (seasonal opening)
Tel. 01423-711147

Royal Baths Assembly Rooms, Crescent Road **Harrogate** HG1 2RR
Tel. 01423-537300

Minster Road **Ripon** HG4 1LT (seasonal opening)
Tel. 01765-604625

Yorkshire & Humberside Tourist Board
312 Tadcaster Road, York YO2 2HF
Tel. 01904-707961

Yorkshire Dales Society
Otley Civic Centre, Cross Green, Otley LS21 1HD
Tel. 01943-607868

The National Trust Regional Office
Goddards, 27 Tadcaster Road, York YO2 2QG
Tel. 01904-702021

National Rail Enquiry Line Tel. 0345-484950

Harrogate & District Travel (bus services)
42 Station Parade, Harrogate HG1 1TX
Tel. 01423-566061

RIPLEY to PATELEY BRIDGE

Distance: 14 miles/22½km

Map:
1:50,000
Landranger 99 - Northallerton & Ripon
1:25,000
Explorer 26 - Nidderdale (to be re-numbered)

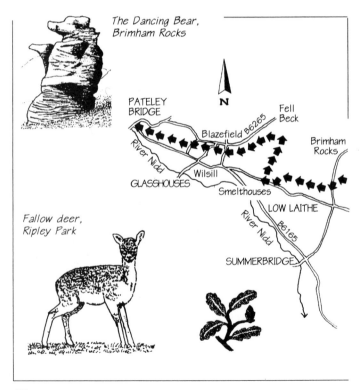

The Dancing Bear, Brimham Rocks

N

PATELEY BRIDGE
Blazefield
Fell Beck
Brimham Rocks
River Nidd
Wilsill
GLASSHOUSES
Smelthouses
LOW LAITHE
River Nidd
SUMMERBRIDGE
B6265
B6165

Fallow deer, Ripley Park

➡ **Start from the market cross and stocks outside the *Boars Head* in the village centre.** Ripley exudes character and breathes history. It was a market town in 1357, and has been the manorial seat of the Ingilby family since before that. Nothing here is without interest, though the castle is the the major draw. First sight is the imposing early 15th century gatehouse: through its great arch are spacious lawns and a courtyard. The castle itself was largely rebuilt in 1555, and much enlarged in 1780, though the old tower is little newer than the gatehouse. After the battle of Marston Moor this Royalist castle supposedly received a visit from Oliver Cromwell, while his troops shot Royalist prisoners they had brought to the village. The lakes and deer park were laid out by Capability Brown, these magnificent grounds being open daily throughout the year. The castle itself is also open at various times during the year, and daily in high summer. It is well worth a visit for both its splendid interior and the contents within.

The village is an attraction in its own right, with numerous shops, a farm museum and a tearoom at the castle. This classic estate village was rebuilt by Sir William Amcotts Ingilby in 1827, based on a French village of Alsace Lorraine - note the old Town Hall named the Hotel de Ville. The medieval market cross has stocks alongside, while a war memorial stands in similar shape. The church was built in 1400 but restored in 1862, and the Ingilby chapel has life-size effigies of Sir Thomas and Lady Ingilby dating from around 1370. In its yard is a pre-

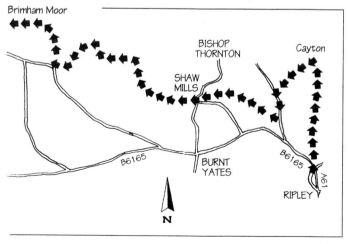

Reformation weeping cross: sockets at the bottom cater for the knees of four penitent souls, and are far from comfortably positioned. After a 70 year lapse, a licensed house was restored to the village in 1990. Inevitably, the *Boars Head* features on the Ingilby crest.

Head north along the main street past the *Boars Head*, and towards the end bear left along a closed road to join the B6165. Prior to Ripley being by-passed this sidelined road was the main road: today it is a 'permissive' route, for which we must tug our forelocks to the Ripley Castle estate. Note, on stepping onto it, an old milestone complete with hands pointing *to Pateley* and *to Ripon*. If a late start demands speedy progress, then a glance at the map reveals that 2 of the first 3 circuitous miles can be omitted by following the B6165 and branching off to pick up the Way at Scarah Bank. **Cross the Pateley Bridge road with care and head off along the steadily rising cul-de-sac of Birthwaite Lane.** This affords extensive views over gently rolling countryside and back to Harrogate on the skyline.

When the road becomes unsurfaced keep straight on to a fork at a triangle. Bear right here, and over the cattle-grid just beyond, bear left. This less firm track runs along the field top becoming a pleasant promenade alongside Sir Henry Wood. At the end remain on this improving bridleway as it curves right in front of another wood. There are now even wider views eastwards across the Vale of York to the North York Moors. **The track slants down the wooded bank to a gate at the bottom, on the grassy floor of Cayton Gill. Just a little further, the now faint way turns to cross the floor of this shallow valley by way of a modest low arched bridge over the stream trickling out of the marsh.**

Ripley Cross

Rising to a gate up the other side, a path then bears left along the top of a newly planted bank before dropping down through two bridle-gates at the end. The path then advances along the edge of this 'dry' valley floor. Grassy mounds up to the right recall the medieval village of Cayton, now only appreciated, if at all, when long evening shadows fall. **Faced with a wood at the end, bear left above marshy ground to a bridle-gate in the far corner. From it turn left to stepping-stones on the little stream, then rise away on a solid access track.** Though depicted as woodland on the map, most of the slopes in this no-man's-land are decorated with vegetation such as bracken and foxgloves.

The cart track runs a leafy course to meet the Ripley-Sawley road. Turn left for five minutes, dropping down Scarah Bank and escaping at the first chance on a farm road to the right. This doubles back to run on into the valley of Thornton Beck. Pass left of the buildings at Low Kettle Spring, and a cart track runs on into trees. A bridleway takes over, rising through trees to approach High Kettle Spring. Avoid this farm by swinging left on a grassy way along the top of the wooded bank, which quickly drops away again. Ahead are fine views over this pleasant side valley to the settlement of Shaw Mills.

In the big field at the bottom of the bank, bear right with the wall. From the left-hand of two gates at the end, rise up the fieldside, remaining with the right-hand boundary after a gate at the top. At a path junction part way along, the Nidderdale Way is signed down to the left. A faint green way descends with the base of a former wall, and at the bottom turn right on the wall-side. Part way through the second field bear gently right, slanting up towards the houses ahead. A wall-stile admits to a small paddock, and a stile admits onto the road on the edge of Shaw Mills. Turn left past the Wesleyan Methodist Church and School of 1904 to the village centre.

The village grew as housing for workers at nearby High Mill, and takes its name from an early millowner. Regretfully, however, the *Nelson Arms* at the heart of this tiny village has fallen a little short of two centuries of serving ale, and in 1998 was derelict, awaiting intended change of use to a private house, an unfortunate sign of the times. A desperate state of affairs indeed, particularly as this was the only pub on the entire stage between Ripley and Pateley Bridge. The environs of the bridge make a delightful floral display with old steps down to Thornton Beck, so it seems we'll just have to drink that in.

Across the bridge turn sharp right along the drive rising to Cowgate Farm. Over to the right, note the sizeable High Mill. Advance straight on between the buildings, and at the last barn the firm track turns left through a gate to pass a house. After this it turns sharp right and runs on as a fieldside track. Adhere to this, ignoring a bridleway left as this track runs on outside a wood. At a gate by a ruin the track completely fades, so from here angle gently down the sloping pasture. There is a glimpse of High Mill's old pond through the trees. At the far bottom corner use a splendid stepped stile built into the wall.

Head away with the wall past a double spring filling a stone trough, just after which is a small gate in the wall. Through it, a footbridge crosses Thornton Beck and a path rises to a stile into a field. Bear left up the fieldside past Beck House (Black House on the map) to a stile onto the drive. This rises away to a T-junction, where turn left along the road which soon descends to the former Woodfield Mill. At the fork at the mill's gateway there is a short-lived choice of routes.

The bridleway descends to the mill. Around 200 years old, it lay derelict before being converted into a fine dwelling. Pass along the front and continue on a green way to rejoin the upper track which runs on to Woodfield House. From a gate to its right rise up the field towards Woodfield Farm, but at a bridleway crossroads bear left to the nearby wall corner. An alternative permissive route follows the upper track behind the mill, then forks right over a cattle-grid on a drive approaching Woodfield Farm: at another cattle-grid the way bears left across the field to pick up the route at a wall corner.

A track descends the wallside to a bridge on Thornton Beck, from where a grassy track climbs the wallside behind. Crossing over the wall at a gate it rises and runs along to meet a drive with Park House just to the right. Turn left, winding through a belt of woodland up to Brimham Lodge. Take the track to the right of the main buildings into the yard at the front. Look left to appraise the remarkable facade of this lovely house dating from the 1660s, on the site of a grange of Fountains Abbey and boasting an astonishing array of mullioned windows. Outside its garden wall, a flight of stone steps mount a sturdy base supporting a stone shaft into which an old sundial is set.

The drive leads out onto the bend of a road, here turn sharp right on a pleasant byway. The track emerges onto the open pasture of Riva Hill, and runs on to join a farm road. Bear left on this under gentle slopes, and as it swings in to Riva Hill Farm, keep straight on an

engaging green way through dense vegetation to a gate/stile onto Brimham Moor. A similar path heads directly away, soon striding out through rolling heather. Though of modest extent, this National Trust access land appears much greater as it sweeps away to the right. Further across, some of the famous rocks rise from bracken and wooded surrounds. **If the day be quiet, arrival on the road crossing the moor is a sudden surprise, being seen only yards before emerging onto it. The entrance to Brimham Rocks is just 100 yards to the right.**

The Druid's Writing Desk

Brimham Rocks are the pride of Nidderdale, a startling collection of gritstone outcrops weathered into innumerable weirdly sculpted shapes. From the car park a broad carriageway leads directly to Brimham House. Formerly the Rocks House, it was built in 1792 by Lord Grantley for his moor keeper, and now serves as a shop and information point, with all the usual National Trust aromas. Refreshments and toilets are also in evidence. A good hour is worth allowing for even the most casual potter round. Ideally, follow the main path round to the left of the house to identify some splendid outcrops, including some of the better known such as the Dancing Bear and Idol Rock (see page 1); then return from the house by way of a meandering path through the myriad boulders above the western scarp. A hundred offshoots seek out the hidden delights in this natural wonderland, where the activities of rock climbers and the extensive Nidderdale views add even further interest.

The Way turns left along the road, and over a brow. Ahead, the celebrated/infamous 'golf balls' of the tracking station at Menwith Hill make a weird apparition. **As the road drops off the moor, turn sharp right on a bridleway. This swings right beneath colourful Brimham country to a gate. A delectable green way drops away into High Wood before emerging into the open.** This opens up the first glorious views over Nidderdale, looking to Guise Cliff under the moorland of High Crag Ridge. **The way becomes enclosed to descend in delightful fashion.** This archetypal green byway still exudes the atmosphere of a monks' trod, one of many cross-country trade routes radiating from Fountains Abbey. **Ultimately it joins a drive, which drops left past the attractive buildings at Low Wood House onto a road at Wysing House. Turn right to drop more steeply into Smelthouses.**

Smelthouses is a charming hamlet in a setting to match. An assortment of graceful dwellings stand near the beck, where as early as the 14th century, ore was brought from nearby lead mines for smelting by the monks of Fountains Abbey. These were joined by several flax mills, including possibly the earliest in the district, in 1798. It is difficult to visualise this sequestered spot as a hive of activity. **Cross the bridge and advance a few yards to find an enclosed path heading off right. Beneath a massive retaining wall it enters Low Wood, commencing**

an enchanting section as the path shadows Fell Beck upstream. Part of the way traces a long-abandoned mill-race. **Above a weir a footbridge leads across the stream at a red-brick hut, and the path doubles back up to the right. Before reaching a larger brick building, turn sharp left on a splendid grassy path through this lovely birchwood.**

On the Panorama Walk, looking across the Nidd to Guise Cliff

Within 150 yards take a branch to the right, a clear path which runs on through the bracken-cloaked woodland floor to an open pasture within the wood: just up to the right are the isolated buildings of Low Wood. The path crosses to a stile back into the trees, and runs on again through abundant holly to a path junction at the end of another woodland 'pasture' just above. Note that both pastures are shown as woodland on the map. The path runs on further than the map suggests, before dropping to a footbridge on Fell Beck. Cross it to leave the wood, and turn right up a cart track.

Within yards the track reaches a crossroads. Just down to the left is Fell Beck Mill, still in operation into the 1960s but now a dwelling. Take the upper track on the left, running into a field. At once leave it by slanting across the field to a gateway, then up the wallside to a gap-stile at the top. Looking back, Brimham Rocks break the skyline across this side valley. Continue up the narrow pasture to the left side of the short terrace of houses at the top. Here take an enclosed leafy way to the left, broadening out with good views over Fell Beck's side valley before reaching a junction of ways above a farm at White Houses.

Cross to a gate opposite from where an initially thin path heads away with a wall, improving as it runs beneath a colourful bank. This is a superb section, with further excellent views over the main valley to Guise Cliff: beneath it is dense woodland, above it heather moorland. The way gently declines before meeting the end of an old drive above a curiously sited modern house. This grassy old way runs on to join a back road on a hairpin bend. Turn uphill 150 yards until a junction appears further above, then turn left along a narrow, enclosed byway. This runs on to meet another back road, which is followed down to the left. As it turns to drop more steeply into Glasshouses, bear right along a bridle-road.

The way runs on past the houses of Blazefield to emerge onto the B6265 Ripon-Pateley Bridge road, where turn downhill once again. An old milestone is passed advising the distances to Skipton, Pateley and Ripon. Again leave along a leafy bridleway on the right, ascending steadily to a junction. Bear left to merge into a drive, running out to the surfaced access road at the exclusive hamlet of Knott. Advance straight on, and at the end bear left on a narrow surfaced way. This is the start of the Panorama Walk, whose long narrow decline leads directly into Pateley Bridge.

The Panorama Walk is a popular local promenade, and part way along, an iron gate admits to a traditional viewing station on a craggy knoll. The ubiquitous Guise Cliff features strongly directly across the valley, with Yorke's Folly silhouetted. Also, Gouthwaite Reservoir makes its first Nidderdale Way appearance ahead: with moorlands beyond, even Great Whernside slots in on the horizon.

The urbanised path slants ever down to pass alongside the cemetery, just before which a snicket runs along to the old church of St. Mary. Embowered in trees in high altitude seclusion, this roofless church dates from the 13th century. It was replaced by the parish church of

St. Cuthbert in the 19th century, and saved from complete ruin as a sister's memorial to her brother in 1906. Before joining the road, the Panorama Walk passes an inscribed stone tablet over an old well on the right. **At the road, turn right to descend the bustling main thoroughfare into the centre of Pateley Bridge.**

Pateley Bridge - Kenaresforde in Domesday is a busy little town, the undisputed 'capital' of Nidderdale. It draws from far and wide: to Nidderdale folk it is the hub of dale life, to visitors from further afield, the first stop. It is literally the key to the upper dale, for all intent on exploring these finest, wilder reaches will pass through here first. Within the town itself are several pubs and cafes, an information centre, buses down-dale to Harrogate, a riverside park, innumerable shops hidden down inviting narrow alleys, and the award-winning Nidderdale Museum. On display here are over 4000 items of life gone by. Unfortunately most of Pateley's industry comes within its scope, for at one time railways, lead mining and quarrying could be added to the more durable farming. At Pateley, too, there is always the river, and the Nidd's banks carry paths in both directions.

Across the bridge at the foot of the High Street are the grounds of Bewerley Park, where the prestigious Nidderdale Show (which is a continuation of the Feast of St Mary, dating from 1320 when a market charter was granted) is held in September, and a regular local auction mart throughout the year. The hall itself, then seat of the Yorke family, was rebuilt in 1820 but demolished a century later. The Yorke name crops up throughout Nidderdale, incidentally, after their acquisition of the estates of Byland Abbey at the Dissolution.

Pateley Bridge

Opposite:
The old church
of St. Mary

PATELEY BRIDGE TO MIDDLESMOOR

Distance: 14½ miles/23km

Map:
1:50,000
Landranger 99 - Northallerton & Ripon
1:25,000
Explorer 26 - Nidderdale (to be re-numbered)

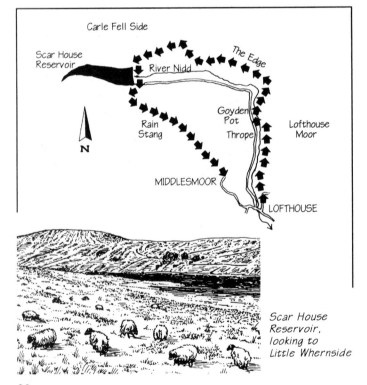

Scar House
Reservoir,
looking to
Little Whernside

Leave the town by turning upstream on a short driveway on the near side of the bridge. At the end a path squeezes through trees to join the Nidd alongside a weir, simply continue upstream. More than 14 miles into the Nidderdale Way, this is its first taste of the riverbank. The ensuing section sees the unsung river at its finest, a lovely stroll along its tree-lined bank. Part-way along, note the lively confluence caused by the arrival of Foster Beck, where a green island sits in the centre of things.

At a wooded corner, clear evidence of an old railway is encountered. The Nidd Valley Light Railway was opened in 1908 by Bradford Corporation to convey material and men for the construction of the Angram dam at the dalehead. It also operated for two decades as a passenger line as far as Lofthouse, but completion of the Scar House

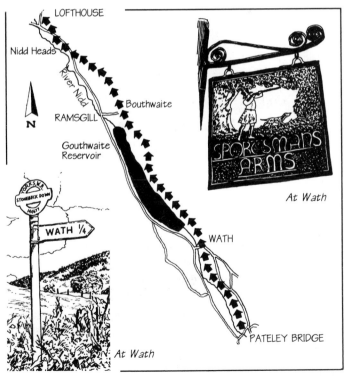

At Wath

At Wath

dam in 1936 saw the end of its useful life. **Emerging at a stile, forsake the riverbank and head directly off along the grassy embankment of the old line. This leads merrily through the fields in peaceful surrounds, and on approaching Wath the path forsakes the line for a wall-stile to the left. Across a further field, a footbridge on a sidestream leads onto the minor road at Wath.**

Just to the left, and linking with the valley road, Wath Bridge stands embowered in greenery. Widened over a century ago, it maintains sufficient character to recall the days when it served the monks of Fountains Abbey and the packhorse trade.

Along to the right, the sleepy hamlet of Wath enjoys a leafy setting of great charm: it is a desperate shame that there are no rights of way by which to explore the hills and gills of its hinterland. Just past the old station house is the *Sportsmans Arms Hotel*, which appropriately enough sports a fine individual sign.

Wath Bridge

Ignoring both bridge and hamlet, take a stile opposite to resume upstream with the Nidd, a short-lived but utterly charming section. At the next stile a section of Gouthwaite's dam appears, and the path crosses the centre of a field to enter trees. A stile and gate lead to a locked gate at the eastern end of the dam. Constructed in 1901, this 80-foot high dam is well camouflaged by foliage, which sets the scene for this least intrusive of the Nidderdale reservoirs. A mostly naturally wooded shoreline masks the harshness of man's hand: indeed, it could be argued that this is merely a return to colder times, when a glacial lake filled the dale floor here.

Take a stile opposite and a grassy trackway rises across two fields to join a firm track. Already there are superb views across Gouthwaite's silvery waters, with patchwork fields and farms beneath a moorland skyline. **Following the track left, it soon descends almost to the very shore of the reservoir, separated only by the green line of the old railway.** Profuse notices make it clear that the inviting trackbed is out of bounds: someone who has just written a whopping cheque for their water rates might view the matter differently. The reason however is that this is an important nature reserve, a favourite habitat of a variety of waterfowl and a birdwatcher's paradise. As the walk progresses, the great advantage of binoculars will become apparent.

Our own track runs a pleasant course parallel with the line for much of the length of Gouthwaite, the only deviation being to the characterful grouping of farm buildings at Covell Houses. On the approach, Ramsgill church is seen beyond the reservoir head, with Middlesmoor on its hilltop site beyond. Covell Houses is an ancient settlement mentioned in Domesday, and at one time a grange of Fountains Abbey. **The route keeps to the left of the buildings and follows the farm road out to the hamlet of Bouthwaite at the head of the reservoir.** The reedy head of the reservoir can be most rewarding for bird sightings, and a fenced viewpoint with a seat is a good location for a break.

At Bouthwaite, note a still working 'Pateley Bridge' clock on the outbuilding opposite. Fountains Abbey - only a few miles distant - had an important grange here, at Ramsgill's smaller neighbour. It is interesting to note that while Nidderdale was in the grip of monastic landlords, it was shared by two abbeys that often had their differences: what they did agree on, by and large, was access on routes across Fountains' land to enable Byland monks and workers to reach their Ramsgill grange and their possessions on the western side of the valley. *LINK ROUTE: A left turn at this crossroads of lanes leads to Nidd Bridge on the edge of Ramsgill, passing en route Bouthwaite Methodist Church (a Bethel Wesleyan Chapel of 1890), and the former station house by the course of the railway.*

At Bouthwaite go right a handful of yards and along an access track bearing right between cottages to enter a farmyard. On the left stands Bouthwaite Grange, a lovely old house with a 1673 datestone and mullioned windows. **From a gate at the end cross a wooden farm bridge on Lul Beck, then bear right to a wall-stile beneath the**

wooded environs of the beck. Rise outside the trees to a stile above, then head away with the wall on the left. An uncomplicated stroll now runs a direct course to Longside Farm, several fields ahead. This section enjoys views back down the valley to Gouthwaite Reservoir, while a substantial length of the old railway line is clearly discernible in the fields below. Middlesmoor is well seen on its tongue of land between the Nidd and How Stean Beck, with flat-topped Little Whernside prominent above the latter valley.

Pass along the rear of the buildings to a gate where its drive is joined. The map shows the Way looping up the field and back down a track, but this is a pointless exercise. Keep straight on the level track, and at the next gate follow it up towards Longside House. From 1968 to 1983 this was a superbly sited youth hostel, but its demise underlines the 'unfashionable' face of Nidderdale. The views from this neighbourhood are truly magnificent, both up and down dale, and across to the moors above Ramsgill.

Passing between the rear of the house and the trees, the path runs on the base of the wood to the far end. It crosses a bracken pasture to a gate in the bottom corner, then drop down to a gate in the fence below. A field track slants down to a gate/stile in the corner below, where the old railway leads out onto the valley road: use a bridle-gate beyond the big gate. Cross to a stile opposite and resume on the course of the old line. In the second field bear right off its embankment to a wall-stile by an old railway box, then continue to another stile just across the corner. Bear left to a gap between wall and trees at a small old quarry, and a track runs the final yards back to the road (stile to the left of the gate).

Turn left along the road for 250 yards to arrive at Nidd Heads. Look over the wall to locate the true river returning to daylight at a rocky door (see page 3), after plunging underground two miles further up-dale - of which more shortly. **Lofthouse is now just two minutes ahead, and the road might be preferred to the designated route, which encounters a potential quagmire. The Way leaves the road directly above Nidd Heads, a path rising to a stile into a field. Cross to a stile in the direction of the village, and on to a gateway. The suspect section awaits: immediately across it take a stile in the adjacent wall, and cross the field to a stile into the village centre between the institute and hotel car parks.** Note the 1653 datestone on a house opposite.

Lofthouse is a small, tidy cluster of stone cottages high above the river, focal point being the attractive corner which includes the homely Post office and a water fountain which bears words well worth reading. The *Crown Hotel* refreshes visitors, while the little school serves all of the upper dale's young-sters. Alongside the school and toilets on the bottom road is the former station house, which was the highest on the Nidd Valley Light Railway.

The Fountain, Lofthouse

Turn right to pass through the top end of the village and out on the moorland road to Masham. This is the only exit from the valley above Pateley Bridge, and was only made fit for motor traffic in the 1960s. **After shrugging off the last houses the road climbs steeply away. Before the first bend, however, leave it by the level track of Thrope Lane along to the left, which runs an unerring, mile-long course to Thrope Farm.** This gem of a byway remains near-level as it parallels the Nidd below, and its general ambience exudes an aura of history. On emerging from trees part way on, the upper dale bursts upon the scene. Thrope had its own watermill until a century ago, and is the site of a small grange of Fountains Abbey. Immediately on reaching it, note the church-like appearance of an up-market shooting house on Thrope Edge high above.

Remain on the track past the farm to gradually drop to the stony course of the river, or more likely its dry bed. Continue 100 yards upstream to Dry Wath, a suitable name for the ford we use to cross to a gate. A good path continues beyond it, soon re-entering the wooded confines of the curving river bed. When a stile returns this old way to the fields, it rises to join the drive to Limley Farm. Follow it into the farmyard. This attractive grouping of stone buildings is on the site of another grange, this time of Byland Abbey.

Just a little further upstream, and well worth the few minutes' detour, is the Nidderdale landmark of Goyden Pot. To see it take a gate to the left of the farm buildings to follow a path on the grassy west bank - if there is some water flowing here, it will be from the inflowing Limley Gill, which is quickly crossed. As the way opens out just beyond, the dark hole of Goyden Pot is found in a crook of the river bed. In normal conditions the Nidd quietly departs underground at Manchester Hole, a further five minutes upstream, but when the flow of water is sufficiently strong the excess is carried down to this point. The river enjoys a subterranean course before re-emerging at Nidd Heads. While the main chamber of Goyden Pot can easily be entered, the inner depths contain a maze of passages best left to the well-equipped, many of whom frequent this locale in their rubber suits and minibuses.

At Limley Farm, head through the yard behind the house, turning first right and then left to pass round the buildings. Behind the last barn a path drops down from a farm track through a nettle-field to cross the dry river bed to a gate. Beyond it the path advances with a collapsed wall, past a barn to join a track which zigzags up the bracken of a steep wooded bank. At the top it leads to a gate to enter the confines of Thwaite House. Originally a grange of Fountains Abbey, this lovely house was saved from decay only a few years ago. Refreshments might be available here, and a 'Ramblers Relief' round the back features pigeons and a charity box - a nice touch.

Pass to the left of the buildings and head off along the access track, soon emerging into more open country for a wide, contouring loop around to the farm of Bracken Ridge. This section boasts particularly spacious views of the upper dale, in both directions; the tree-lined river winds below, while the dam of Scar House Reservoir appears

Haytime near Thrope Farm

26

under Little Whernside. **At Bracken Ridge there is no need to enter the yard.** Note, however, the lovely old barn at the top side, featuring mullioned windows. **Remain on the track which climbs above the farm to commence a lengthy traverse of The Edge.**

This broad track is a splendid platform along which several farms and cottages are based, taking advantage of the spring line, which is in evidence at several locations along the way. Looking ahead, Little Whernside is joined by the northern shoulder of Great Whernside. **With a wall to the left and steep slopes to the right, the track runs on pleasurably to New Houses Edge Farm, the last settlement on The Edge.** Only on approaching here does Great Whernside's actual summit slot in to place at the dalehead.

Beyond the farm the track fords a stream and enters an open pasture. Just a little further it forks: remain on the more inviting upper branch, a green way running on to cross a bracken pasture. Towards the bottom bear right at a fork to climb by a tiny stream. The track maintains a steep pull through bracken-cloaked slopes before swinging left at a steady angle. A hairpin bend is encountered on reaching a wall corner. At this point the waters of Scar House are visible for the first time above the dam wall.

The map depicts the bridleway maintaining its slant through the wall in front, but this has never been the case. Instead, remain on the grassy track which winds up to a gate higher up. Here open moorland is entered, and the firm course of the track fades. A series of marker posts guide a fainter path across to the left, rising gently to quickly merge into a Landrover track. Ahead, the dam of the higher level Angram Reservoir has appeared beyond the waters of Scar House. **The track quickly descends to cross Twizling Gill and the deeper, bracken-choked confines of Woo Gill in quick succession.**

Climbing away, keep to the upper track which runs on to a gate above a small plantation, then encounters marshy ground to continue along the flank of Carle Fell. It slants down to cross a firm track just before a second one above the dam of Scar House Reservoir. Immediately below is a rest house, a quaint facility provided by the old water board, and certainly appreciated if caught by a sudden shower. Scar House Reservoir, with its partner Angram Reservoir, fills the head of Nidderdale. Scar House was completed in 1936 by Bradford Corporation, and boasts a masonry dam rising 150 feet.

Across the valley, below the car park, can be seen the site of the temporary village that existed during the construction years: here was a complete settlement, with little short of 100 children schooled here in the 1920s. On the hillsides, meanwhile, are the quarries opened specifically to win stone for the dams. Everything was on site, including, no doubt, very soon the water! **Turn down to follow the road along the top of the dam: this is, in every sense, the turning point of the Way.** Along to the left is a large car park with picnic area and toilets. This is the terminus of a private Water Company road from Lofthouse, open to traffic with a toll payable at the entrance. **The Nidderdale Way, meanwhile, turns sharp right on an access road.**

Just before a gate and sidestream, double back left up a firm track. This makes a short ascent of steep, rocky slopes before easing out on the moor. Pause to look back over this great sweep of the majestically wild upper reach of Nidderdale, with Great and Little Whernsides encircling the reservoir: Great Whernside's rippling shoulders form a comprehensive barrier to the dalehead, making it difficult to imagine that such a cosy village as Kettlewell could be only a couple of miles down its other flank. Directly opposite are the extensive former Carle Side Quarries. Our route is the old road from Middlesmoor to Coverdale by way of the Lodge, a ruin identified by a clump of trees far across the water. Its approach to the Lodge was drowned by the construction of the reservoir, and its purpose further diminished by construction of the road on the bed of the Nidd Valley Light Railway.

On the ascent to Rain Stang, looking back over Scar House Reservoir to Carle Side and the extensive quarry remains

The track runs on across the moorland of Rain Stang. This brief stride enjoys the bleakest setting of any section of the Way, with nothing other than rolling, open country to survey. Quite appropriate too, as just ahead the Nidderdale Way reaches its highest elevation. With Scar House gone, Gouthwaite Reservoir surprisingly bursts onto the scene far down the valley. **The old road quickly becomes enclosed to encounter the summit of the walk at 1427ft/435m. From this point a long, steady descent of the stony In Moor Lane leads unfailingly down into Middlesmoor.** About half a mile before the end, at a water company installation, note a weathered old milestone on the right.

Middlesmoor is Nidderdale's first village. Its name accurately describes its position, on a broad tongue between the valley of the Nidd and its major tributary How Stean Beck. The homely *Crown Inn* and adjacent former Post office occupy a particularly attractive corner across from the old school. This bears an 1869 datestone, but an older tablet informs of its endowment in 1803 and building in 1807. An intricate network of alleyways wind between gritstone

cottages with flowery gardens to the church of St. Chad. Rebuilt in 1866, it stands on an ancient foundation: a Saxon cross within is said to have been the 7th century preaching cross of St. Chad. It is better known, perhaps, as a viewpoint, for the churchyard provides a foreground to what is a renowned panorama down the length of the dale, to Gouthwaite Reservoir and beyond.

St. Chad's, Middlesmoor

STAGE 3

MIDDLESMOOR to BEWERLEY

Distance: 10½ miles/17km

Map:
1:50,000
Landranger 99 - Northallerton & Ripon
1:25,000
Explorer 26 - Nidderdale (to be re-numbered)

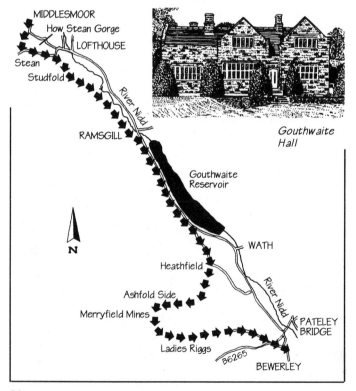

Gouthwaite
Hall

MIDDLESMOOR
How Stean Gorge
LOFTHOUSE
Stean
Studfold
River Nidd
RAMSGILL
Gouthwaite
Reservoir
N
WATH
Heathfield
Ashfold Side
River Nidd
Merryfield Mines
PATELEY
BRIDGE
Ladies Riggs
B6265
BEWERLEY

▶ **Middlesmoor is left by the road descending steeply out of the village past a former Wesleyan chapel of 1899. Opposite a barn, take a stile on the right. Descend two field-sides, with the hamlet of Stean across the slopes just opposite. A stile part-way down the next field sends a path slanting down to the top of the tree-lined confines of the ravine of How Stean Beck. Descending to a footbridge the path climbs onto the back road serving the hamlet of Stean, just above. Go left on the narrow road which runs quickly along to the entrance to How Stean Gorge, passing How Stean Tunnel on the right.**

A visit to How Stean Gorge is an event to remember, and it is well worth taking the time to savour its delights. An entrance fee is payable at the cafe, which has a gift shop, toilets, and peacocks patrolling the grounds. How Stean Gorge is a marvellous natural spectacle, a limestone ravine half a mile long and up to 80 feet deep. The rocks have been worn into some dramatic contours by the action of the swift-flowing water, and deep, dark and wet caves abound. The entire expedition is but a short one, the part downstream from the cafe being especially exciting as the path crosses dramatically suspended bridges to guarded natural walkways through the rocks. Of further interest are How Stean Tunnel, near the walk's upper limit, and Tom Taylor's Chamber, where Roman coins were unearthed in the 19th century. This 530ft cave runs from the gorge to the field behind the cafe, and even novice troglodytes are able to negotiate it with the aid of a torch hired from the cafe.

How Stean Gorge

Back out on the road, follow this down to where it bridges How Stean Beck. *LINK ROUTE: Lofthouse is 5 minutes over the bridge.* **Without crossing, advance straight along the road to Studfold Farm.** Like Stean earlier, here was a small grange of Byland Abbey, while today an outdoor centre and a caravan site (small shop) share the farming environs. **Turn sharp right up the steep, rough road to a line of cottages, where escape left on another walled track. This runs on to cross Blayshaw Gill before emerging into a field. While the access track climbs to High Blayshaw Farm, the Way advances straight along a more inviting green track to a stile/gate.**

With the benefit of contouring across the valley flanks, all of this section enjoys spacious views up-dale to Lofthouse, Middlesmoor and beyond: a superb panorama. **The way slants gently right towards a barn, beyond which it runs as a firmer track through the fields to**

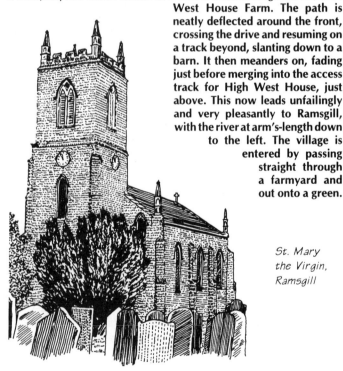

West House Farm. The path is neatly deflected around the front, crossing the drive and resuming on a track beyond, slanting down to a barn. It then meanders on, fading just before merging into the access track for High West House, just above. This now leads unfailingly and very pleasantly to Ramsgill, with the river at arm's-length down to the left. The village is entered by passing straight through a farmyard and out onto a green.

*St. Mary
the Virgin,
Ramsgill*

32

Ramsgill is the showpiece village of the upper dale, on the banks of its own beck just short of its confluence with the Nidd. Prime feature is the spacious green, where attractive cottages and flowery gardens play support to the imposing ivy-clad hotel (see page 48). Since extended, the *Yorke Arms* is a former shooting lodge still bearing the name of its one-time occupants. A circular stone pinfold stands in front of the village hall. In earlier times Ramsgill was an important grange of Byland Abbey, and at the rear of the church a solitary gable-end is all that remains of the monks' chapel. The solid looking church was rebuilt in 1843, and looks out across the reedy head of Gouthwaite Reservoir.

After a sojourn on the green, continue south on the road out of the village. Gouthwaite Reservoir returns, and the road clings to its shore for two winding miles. Though this is not an entirely satisfactory arrangement, there are no rights of way other than the outward route on the opposite shore. Despite being neither an A or B road, nor a through route of any note, it attracts more than an occasional vehicle as it serves the communities of the upper dale, so take care. It does, however, enjoy superb views over the reservoir, with several refuges provided for birdwatching.

Ultimately the road passes the striking frontage of Gouthwaite Hall. This is a 1901 replacement (including some original stonework) for the former seat of the Yorke family which had to make way for the reservoir. **Around the next corner, a narrow, winding strip of tarmac climbs away from the road at a cattle-grid.** Unsignposted and resembling a private drive, it affords extensive views back over the reservoir and further up-dale. **Passing through the dense West Wood, the road levels out to arrive at a fork at the scattered group of dwellings at Heathfield.**

This ancient settlement once had a fulling mill under the auspices of the monks of Byland Abbey, while the ubiquitous Yorke family smelted ore here from their lead mines. Here the road drops down to the left, with Pateley Bridge appearing at this very point. Just yards further down the road are the attractive Grange Cottage with its mullioned windows, and a contrastingly simple corrugated old chapel. **The Way, however, turns right along the short access road into a cluster of houses. Passing straight through, the track climbs a wooded bank to a cattle-grid at a bend at the top, with the farm of Highfield just above.**

Although the map depicts the route using the public footpath up past the farm, the Way actually follows the easier route of a bridleway. Advance to the gate in front, and head away with a wall on the right. There are sweeping views down-dale to Pateley Bridge and Guise Cliff. From the gate at the bottom descend the field centre towards a barn, and from the right-hand gate descend again to a gate above Spring House Farm. Slant down to the right around the back of extensive outbuildings to a gate between the two stone buildings into the yard. Drop straight down to the right-hand gate below, and descend the fieldside to join a narrow road at the end of a caravan site.

Go right in the company of Ashfold Side Beck, clusters of caravans now appearing with regularity. At a steep fork to Westfield House Farm, remain on the level road into another site. Threading its way through it finally shrugs off the last caravan to become unsurfaced. As a well engineered old mine road it runs along this increasingly attractive side valley of Merryfield Glen. Suddenly and dramatically, old mine workings appear across the beck, and a footpath breaks off to slant down to cross Ashfold Side Beck on a concrete ford.

The Merryfield Mines provide a marvellous insight into the dale's important lead mining past, and the Prosperous Smelt Mill is one of the major sites. The aim is to gain the far upper side of the workings. Behind the large ruinous building which was the smelt mill (note the geared winding shaft in situ) a narrow green path heads half-left, out of the site and slanting up through heather, doubling back to join a level, broader path. Turning right along it, the track runs through the heart of the site, at the foot of the main spoil-heaps. Approaching the wall at the far side turn left, and the track starts to climb above the site, passing one last forlorn ruin. The track levels out beneath a knoll of modest gritstone rocks on Nabs to run on to a gateway, here transferring to the next side valley, that of Brandstone Beck. Note the benchmark on a rock immediately through the gateway.

The track swings left, ignoring a right turn through a gate, and keeping right at a fork to descend to Brandstone Dub Bridge. This shapely structure has an attractive little waterfall just below. The sides of this gill also supported a number of smelting mills. Note the isolated house at Sun Side in the trees on the north bank. Across the bridge head confidently away, soon arriving at Hillend where the track drops down to cross Coldstones Beck. At this junction of ways the lane becomes surfaced. The house up to the right (Low Hole Bottom) operated as Pateley Bridge youth hostel for ten years up to 1956.

After an enclosed spell the lane rises past another farm onto Ladies Riggs. This lofty crest offers outstanding views both up and down the dale, and back over the Way's most recent meanderings. **The road then descends past Riggs House Farm and into a shroud of trees.** *LINK ROUTE: At this point a direct path makes for Pateley Bridge: head through the few trees on the left to a stile in the corner, and with Pateley Bridge in view below, simply follow the right-hand field boundaries downhill onto a back road at Bridgehouse Gate.*

The Way continues straight down the road past Eagle Hall to join the B6265 Grassington-Pateley Bridge road just above Bridgehouse Gate. Cross straight over and down the narrow road opposite to shortly enter Bewerley. Bewerley is a hugely attractive village with carefully tended gardens leading the eye to innumerable cosy cottages. Its celebrated chapel is featured at the start of the next stage.

Prosperous Smelt Mill, Merryfield

35

STAGE 4

BEWERLEY TO RIPLEY

Distance: 14 miles/22½km

Map:
1:50,000
Landranger 99 - Northallerton & Ripon
Landranger 104 - Leeds, Bradford & Harrogate
1:25,000
Explorer 26 - Nidderdale (to be re-numbered)

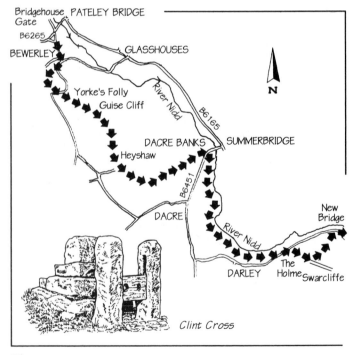

➧ **Head south along the length of Bewerley's broad street, passing Bewerley Grange Chapel on the left.** The chapel was built as part of a grange of Fountains Abbey by Marmaduke Huby, who was Abbot there from 1494-1526: his motto is inscribed on the outside wall. The building was sympathetically restored in 1965, and stands in peaceful grounds (see page 5). **Ignore the first turn right (Peat Lane) and continue down to the junction at Turner Bridge. Bearing right, a choice of ways awaits. The waymarked route stays on the road as it starts to climb, taking a stile on the right and climbing the large field to a stile into the top of Skrikes Wood.**

That highlighted on the map, however, is marginally longer but more rewarding. Take the first turn right at the Skrikes Farm drive, but instead of following it, the diverted path takes a gate on the right, then slants down to Fosse Gill. This leads upstream beneath the farm to enter Skrikes Wood. This magnificent woodland has been designated a nature reserve chiefly for the variety of bird-life it attracts. Just a little further, the path meets a broader one just short of a footbridge. Double back left up this for a mercurial climb through the wood. At a level section half way up, note the prostrate tree on the left, supporting a thriving array of vertical branches. The path then climbs along the wood edge to absorb the direct path coming up the field.

The upper stage of the wood sees the path climb out of the trees, crossing over a green way and rising through colourful vegetation to a stile in the sturdy wall above. The direct path continues straight up through the heather to join the moor road at the top of Nought Bank. This was on the main road to Otley two centuries ago. There are likely to be several cars parked around the lay-by for easy access to Yorke's

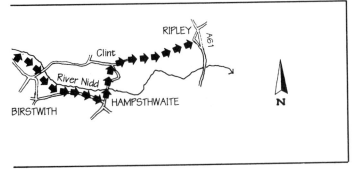

Folly. However, a very short loop from the stile goes left to wind round to the prominent Crocodile Rock: the resemblance is not obvious, but the location can't be challenged, while Elton John fans are likely to break into song at this point. The path then doubles back round to the road, with Yorke's Folly waiting ahead. **Cross straight over the road and along the popular path to the waiting towers of Yorke's Folly.**

Highly prominent in many a Nidderdale scene, Yorke's Folly was built 200 years ago by a member of the Yorke family to provide local employment. Supposed to resemble a Rhineland ruin, it probably does more so since one of the three original towers succumbed to a severe storm in 1893, thereby rendering its hitherto local name of Three Stoops redundant (though 'Two Stoops' still works well!).

Yorke's Folly

Just beyond the folly the path crosses a ladder-stile in the sturdy wall and heads off to follow it along the moor edge. A grand stride leads on above the top end of Guisecliff Wood to a stile in a fence. The footpath shown on the map crossing the moor further south is non-existent on the ground, and the accepted route is that crossing the stile. This begins a classic section as the path runs unerringly along the crest of Guise Cliff, with tempting branches seeking out even more exposed situations.

Below is a wonderful panorama of the dale, seen as on a map beyond the magnificent rock architecture. Children and vertigo sufferers should NOT be near the edge, not only for the all too obvious sheer drop (which falls 100 feet at its peak) but because there are also some mischievous crevices. The blanket of woodland below is so complete as to hide the still waters of the oval Guisecliff Tarn in its midst, though Gouthwaite Reservoir is clearly seen up-dale.

Towards the end leave the bouldery edge, keeping right of the re-formed wall to run on to the big mast that has long been in view. The path is deflected outside its perimeter fence to a junction of ways behind it. Ahead, the Menwith Hill golf balls dramatically appear, overlooking the lower sweep of the valley past Darley and round towards Harrogate. Once again advance straight on, a good track remaining with the wall to arrive above a lone house at High Hood Gap. Absorbing the drive it resumes along the edge of the now rougher moor, passing beneath substantial quarry spoil to wind along to the far corner. Alongside the buildings at Hill Top the Way takes its leave of moorland and the track runs down to enter the hamlet of Heyshaw.

Turning left, the road ends within yards. Advance to a stile by a gate just ahead, then turn right to cross a slim paddock with a farm just to the right. Across the parallel fence, head straight down the field centre away from the farm to a waiting ladder-stile. Below here a grassy track descends several fields to Lanes Foot. En route, the way encounters some sections of old stone causey and a substantial plantation completely ignored by the mapmakers. Pass through a gate into the confines of the two attractive houses and follow the drive out to a crossroads with Monk Ing Road.

Turn left down this farm access road, ignoring the first drive left, to Northwoods. Ahead is the inimitable Brimham Rocks skyline, with Summerbridge in view on the valley side. Continue down to a cattle-grid and stile at the bottom. As the farm road turns left to Eastwoods, bear right down the large field to a wall-stile in the bottom corner, then go right a short way to a stile in the adjacent fence. Curve round the field corner and descend with the wall on the right. From a gate at the bottom corner a track winds down to the farmyard below, at Hill Top. Pass straight through and down its access track.

As the track swings along to the right, now level, look for a kissing-gate on the left. The Way is now on the edge of Dacre Banks. Just ahead is the old school, which gave remarkable service as a youth hostel for more than half a century until its demise in 1987. **Descend the wallside to an unlikely little gate in the bottom corner, which admits to another farmyard. Drop straight down again, continuing down the access road which quickly swings left.** Just along to the right is the long abandoned site of the village railway station. **At this bend take a pathway in front to join the suburban Grange Road, which leads down onto the B6451 in the centre of Dacre Banks. The Way turns left, though the pub is just 100 yards along to the right.** This is a pleasant village with a name and setting to match: just across its triangular green stands the *Royal Oak*, a welcoming pub. If detouring, the route can be rejoined by continuing a few yards past it, down between farm buildings on a track into a field, just across which is the riverbank path.

Leave by heading left on the main road past the secluded church to the arched bridge linking Dacre Banks with Summerbridge. Important note: the latter boasts a chip shop! Immediately upstream is a busy sawmill, where wood arrives from all over to be prepared largely for use in furniture. **Without crossing the bridge, take a stile on the right from where steps send a path downstream, passing well tended sports fields. This next lengthy section is infallible as the Way simply holds tight to the riverbank, for the first time in many miles.**

After a brief detour up above a wooded bank alongside Low Hall, the riverbank walk is pure delight. The observant may glimpse the unforgettable sight of a kingfisher over the water, and during this first mile, pause also to look back at the prospect of Low Hall's splendid facade. Some stones in this Tudor-style house are said to have come from Fountains Abbey. **The path soon has its first encounter with the former Nidd Valley Railway.** The old line is much in evidence on this stage, and the forlorn bridgework of an old underpass is a sad reminder of what must have been a typical rural branch line. The Nidd

Valley Line was opened in 1862 by the North Eastern Railway, largely to serve industry in the dale. It ran from near Harrogate to Pateley Bridge, and its single-track line finally succumbed in 1964, having already been closed to passengers 13 years earlier.

With the old embankment on the right, it is not long before the path enjoys greater freedom as it ambles on past stepping-stones to cross a footbridge over inflowing Darley Beck. Appearing just ahead are the houses of Darley, a linear village whose pub *The Wellington* is unfortunately some way off-route at the western end, as is the large Darley Mill Centre, with its cafe. **The path runs along the garden foots of prestige dwellings on the site of Darley's former railway station, and continues to a footbridge over the river. Ignoring this, turn right a few yards to join a broader track - the old railway again. At this path crossroads turn left, parallel with the river on a muddy track over a farm bridge on a sidestream. Across, rise into the field above and follow the top of the wooded bank, on a pleasant course which squeezes between holly and brambles to emerge at a stile into a field. Head diagonally across a couple of fields to the group of houses at The Holme, where a stile admits onto the road.**

On Guise Cliff, looking over Guisecliff Wood to Glasshouses

Turn left on the footway past these few scattered dwellings on the eastern outskirts of Darley. The thatched Holme Hall is known locally as Darley Laundry, which it operated as at the end of the 19th century. **After the last house take a stile/gate on the right, and cross to the far corner of the field. Head away with the wall, and at the few trees at the end, rise a few yards before crossing a couple more pastures parallel with the road below. Ahead, a stile gives access to a woodland corner, and a path runs on through bracken to meet a rising bridlepath. Turn up into the wood of Reynard Crag, this superb old way being substantially flagged as it climbs through glorious birchwood, a favourite haunt of deer.**

Beyond a gate at the top the path continues in delightful fashion up the side of the wood to emerge onto the end of a lane at Swarcliffe. A holiday park on the right occupies the site of a former slaughterers. **Continue up a little further to Rennie Crag Farm, then turn left along a driveway.** From this high vantage point savour the extensive views back updale, over a great curve of the valley to the higher moors beyond; additionally, Brimham Rocks and Moor are prominent

directly across the dale, while a clear day reveals the long Hambleton Hills skyline on the North York Moors far across the Vale of York. **At the house at the end go straight on down a path into the trees, descending the woodside in similar fashion to the very recent ascent, with fine views ahead over the Birstwith neighbourhood. At the bottom descend a fieldside back onto the road.**

New Bridge, near Birstwith

Turn right for a short while for a gentle rise. There is barely a dwelling in sight amid the valley's outstanding wooded scenery. **At a bend escape down a narrow lane on the left by Birstwith House.** With a farm on the right, note the lovely old house dated 1688 with mullioned windows on the left. **From the gate at the bottom a track continues down, and a footpath takes over to approach the river. Though the route takes a stile on the right, first advance a few yards further to admire the beautiful arch of New Bridge.** Dating from around 1615, it was on the packhorse route from Ripon to Skipton, but was demolished in 1822 and rebuilt 25 yards downstream.

Back at the stile, turn downstream for a delightful short section, soon cutting out a bend of the river as it shadows a hedge outside a cricket pitch. Ahead is the unmistakeable sight of the large animal feeds mill at Birstwith. To the right is the rather more elegant tall spire of Birstwith church, built 1857, while Swarcliffe Hall stands in lovely grounds on the hill above. **At the end the river is rejoined as the way runs on the edge of sports fields to emerge onto the road in Birstwith.** A mill-cut shadows the route out onto the road from a wide weir on the Nidd. Just to the left the river bridge leads to the *Station Hotel*, while Birstwith's most attractive corners (and shop) are along to the right.

The Way crosses straight over the road towards the mill yard. The path has been diverted to the left of the mill, so after re-crossing the mill-cut on a footbridge, shadow the perimeter fence around above the river. At the end turn sharp right with the fence, along to a kissing-gate back onto the original line of the path. Here turn left on a wallside path, and from a stile at the end, rejoin the riverbank. This leads pleasantly downstream again, though the point of leaving it is not obvious. This comes as a barn roof is spotted up to the right: bear up to it where a gate deposits the Way back onto the road. Note the character of this L-shaped old stable block, with a mullioned window but sadly a very modern roof.

Bear left along the road for Hampsthwaite, the 'official' route remaining on the road throughout to enter alongside a small green. Those in no hurry will vary the entry into Hampsthwaite just after the church tower appears ahead. At a bend at the village sign, bear left on a gem of a part-flagged, leafy byway to emerge into the churchyard. The church of St. Thomas a'Becket dates largely from only a century ago, but the tower is a good 500 years old. A path runs along the front of the church and out onto the village street. The village centre is just to the right along Church Lane. Within a stone's throw of the triangular green complete with old village pump, are its various facilities including the *Joiners Arms*. Once a busy market town, Hampsthwaite also marked an important river crossing for the Romans on their road from Ilkley to Aldborough, near Boroughbridge.

The Way turns north from the village green, along Church Lane past the church and over the graceful bridge. This is the moment to bid a fond farewell to the Nidd. A tablet on the other side proudly records the building of a wall to commemorate Queen Victoria's Diamond Jubilee - fascinating! **Head along the roadside footway to the sharp bend ahead.** This is the obvious site of a former bridge on the defunct railway, and is the Nidderdale Way's final railway encounter.

Hampsthwaite Bridge

From the gate in front climb the fieldside. Pause on the brow to appraise one last sweeping prospect of the verdant Nidd Valley, including much of the last stage of the route, with the solid tower of Hampsthwaite church and the Menwith Hill golf balls prominent. **Advance along the wallside to a stile onto the road in Clint.** A detour one hundred yards left up the road finds the ancient Clint Cross, restored in 1977, and adjacent stocks. **Cross straight over and bear right along Hollybank Lane, which will lead all the way back to the walk's conclusion. A lengthy, traffic-free stride along this leafy byway with open views leads to its surfaced demise at isolated Holly Bank Lodge. Keep straight on into Hollybank Wood, perhaps at its finest when carpeted with bluebells.**

The Way emerges as a cart track which maintains a leafy course until Ripley church appears ahead. A broader track is joined and just beyond, the Ripley Castle estate wall is met at another junction. There is the possibility of a glimpse of the fallow deer inside the grounds. **Keep straight on to find the castle itself appearing ahead, and as the way drops downhill, the lake makes a splendid foreground. At the bottom its outflow, Ripley Beck, is bridged and the lane rises into the centre of the village.** Back in the cobbled square, celebratory pints, cuppas or ice creams are all within even a tired man's reach.

The Gatehouse, Ripley Castle

A LOG OF THE WALK

Date	Place	Miles		Notes
		stage	total	
	Ripley	-	-	
	Shaw Mills	4¾	4¾	
	Brimham Rocks	9	9	
	Smelthouses	10	10	
	Blazefield	12½	12½	
	Pateley Bridge	14	14	
	Wath	1¾	15¾	
	Bouthwaite	4¼	18¼	
	Lofthouse	6¼	20¼	
	Scar House	12	26	
	Middlesmoor	14½	28½	
	How Stean Gorge	¾	29¼	
	Ramsgill	3½	32	
	Heathfield	6¼	34¾	
	Bewerley	10½	39	
	Heyshaw	3	42	
	Dacre Banks	5¼	44¼	
	The Holme (Darley)	8	47	
	Birstwith	10¼	49¼	
	Hampsthwaite	11½	50½	
	Ripley	14	53	

Gouthwaite Reservoir

INDEX
Principal features

At Scar House Reservoir

THE NIDDERDALE WAY

Scar House
Reservoir

Nidd

Angram
Res

Middlesmoor

Ramsgill

Lofthouse

Gouthwaite Reservoir

Wath

Nidd

RIPON

PATELEY BRIDGE

Fountains Abbey

Glasshouses

Greenhow
Hill

Bewerley

Smelthouses

Bishop Thornton

Summerbridge

Shaw
Mills

Dacre Banks

River Nidd

Darley

Birstwith

Ripley

Hampsthwaite

*Ramsgill,
featuring the
Yorke Arms*

Blubberhouses

HARROGATE

N